# Be a
# FOSSIL
## DETECTIVE

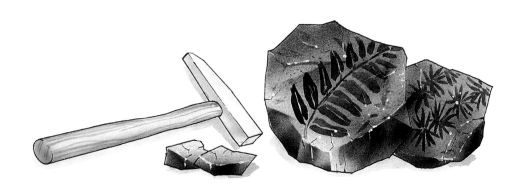

Written by

## Dougal Dixon MSc

Illustrated by

## Chris Forsey

**Derrydale Books**
New York

A TEMPLAR BOOK

First published in 1989 by Derrydale Books
distributed by Crown Publishers, Inc.,
225 Park Avenue South, New York, New York 10003

Devised and produced by Templar Publishing Ltd
Pippbrook Mill, London Road, Dorking, Surrey RH4 1JE

Editors Amanda Wood, Andrew Charman
Designer Peter Marriage
Printed and bound in UK

ISBN 0-517-68022 X

h g f e d c b

# C O N T E N T S

# Time!

The Earth is old. Very, very, old. It is difficult to imagine how old it is. The rocks that make up the Earth are all around us; under our feet wherever we walk and as part of the buildings in which we live. There are three different kinds of rock in the Earth's crust, and you can find out how they are formed on these two pages.

Take a look at the building you're in at the moment. If it is a sandstone building, you will see that it is made of sand, pressed together so that it has solidified into one mass. It is an example of a sedimentary rock.

All around you are examples of the other kinds of rock. Statues that you see in parks and museums are often made of marble, which is a metamorphic rock. Granite, on the other hand, is an example of an igneous rock. It is very hard and lasts a long time, which is why we often use it for building.

## THREE KINDS OF ROCK

There are three kinds of rock in the Earth's crust.

Rocks are broken down into small particles by the wind and rain.

Particles fall to the bottom of the sea, forming layers.

As more layers form, those underneath become compressed.

**Sedimentary rock**. This rock is formed when little pieces of sand or mud collect as layers and are eventually compressed and cemented into a solid mass. Sedimentary rock is a bit like bread and jam. On your bread you could spread a layer of butter. Then you could spread a layer of jam. Finally, you put on another layer of bread and butter. When you bite into your sandwich, you can see the different layers.

Out of these three types of rock, it is sedimentary rock that is important to the fossil hunter. You can find out why on pages 8 and 9.

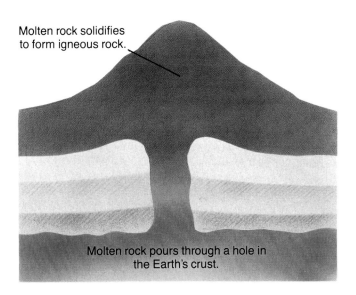

Molten rock solidifies to form igneous rock.

Molten rock pours through a hole in the Earth's crust.

**Igneous rock**. This rock is formed when molten material from inside the Earth cools and solidifies. It is like melting sugar in a pan. If you leave the melted sugar in the pan, it cools and becomes a solid lump of toffee. Molten rocky material cools to form igneous rock in much the same way.

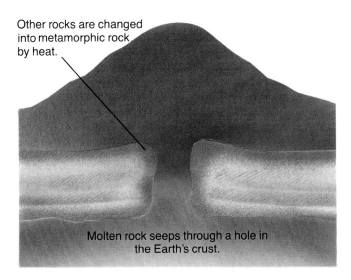

Other rocks are changed into metamorphic rock by heat.

Molten rock seeps through a hole in the Earth's crust.

**Metamorphic rock**. This rock forms when another rock – igneous or sedimentary – is compressed or heated up deep inside the Earth and changes into a completely different rock. It is a bit like putting a cake into an oven. Once the original cake mixture has been cooked, it comes out as a solid cake – quite different in appearance to the gooey mixture you put in.

# What kind of rock is this?

*See if you can guess from the descriptions below to which rock type these three rocks belong.*

①

This rock has been formed over millions of years, as particles of sand and small sea creatures have been pressed together. You can see the individual sand grains in this cross-section.

②

This rock was once a sedimentary rock called limestone. It has been changed by great temperatures in the Earth's crust to form the rock that you can see here.

③

This rock is formed from molten magma, deep inside the Earth. It has cooled slowly and become very hard.

# *Fossil rock!*

*Out of the three types of rock in the Earth's crust, **sedimentary rock** is the most important to the fossil detective. The reason is simple – sedimentary rock is the type most likely to contain fossils. You can see why from the illustrations below.*

**1.** The first layer of sand that ended up as sedimentary rock may have formed in a desert. Animals that live in the desert will have died there and left their remains among the sand.

**2.** Over many years, sea may have spread over the desert, forming a layer of mud on the sea bed. Sea creatures such as fish and crabs would have died and fallen to the bottom of the sea where their remains would have mixed with the mud.

**3.** Next, the sea may have dried up, leaving a shingle beach – the gravel layer. New creatures would have moved in to live here and added their remains to the growing number of layers.

**4.** Finally, rivers may have formed, cutting across the gravel and bringing with them a new layer of sand, and yet more creatures.

River (sand)

Beach (gravel)

Sea (mud)

Desert (sand)

**5.** The materials left behind by each of the stages – the sand, mud and gravel – are called **sediments**. The layers each one formed are called **beds**. Over millions of years the beds would have been compressed and squeezed together. Water seeping through them would have left behind minerals, which were trapped between the grains. These minerals would have cemented the grains and the animal remains among them, into a solid rock. The animal remains are what we know as **fossils**.

## MEASURING TIME

It takes millions of years for sedimentary rock to form. The figures involved are too big for us to handle. So, to make it easier, geologists (people who study rocks) break down the millions of years in the history of the Earth into divisions called **eras** and **periods**.

This chart is called a **geological column**. It gives the eras and periods, with the oldest at the bottom and the youngest at the top, plus the ages in hundreds of millions of years. You will find this column useful to look at when you've read about some of the creatures on the following pages.

| | Millions of years | Today | ERA |
|---|---|---|---|
| CENOZOIC | 2 | Quaternary Period | CENOZOIC |
| MESOZOIC | | Tertiary Period | |
| PALAEOZOIC | 65 | | |
| | | Cretaceous Period *Last dinosaurs* | MESOZOIC |
| | 144 | Jurassic Period | |
| | 213 | | |
| | | Triassic Period *First mammals and dinosaurs* | |
| | 248 | | |
| | | Permian Period | PALAEOZOIC |
| | 286 | | |
| | | Carboniferous Period *First reptiles* | |
| | 360 | | |
| | | Devonian Period *First land animals* | |
| | 408 | Silurian Period *First land plants* | |
| PRECAMBRIAN | 438 | Ordovician Period *First fish* | |
| | 505 | | |
| | | Cambrian Period *Earliest fossils* | |
| *Beginning of the Earth* | 590 | Precambrian | |
| 4500 | | | |

9

# How fossils form

When an animal or plant dies, it eventually disappears. It may be eaten up by scavenging birds and animals like crows, or vultures, or hyenas. It may be eaten up by smaller creatures like beetles and maggots. What is left will normally just rot away and nothing will be left. But sometimes parts of the animal are left behind – like those that got trapped in the rock on the previous page. These may be preserved in the rock as **fossils**.

A dinosaur is killed by another at the edge of a river. Its remains are washed into the water and fall to the river bed.

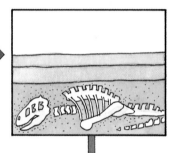

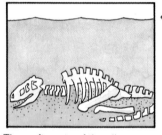

The soft parts of the dinosaur rot away. The hard parts – the bones and teeth – remain stuck in the river bed.

Over time, layers of mud form on the river bed. As more and more layers pile up, the mud hardens into rock. The bones and teeth are trapped inside as fossils. Over thousands of years the river dries up and becomes a desert again. Then sea covers the desert and carves a cliff face in the rock. The fossil bones and teeth are revealed.

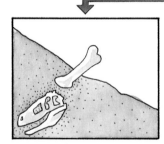

**Original remains.** The bones and teeth may be dug out unchanged.

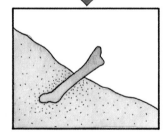

**Petrified fossils!** Sometimes the original cells – the tiny units that fitted together like jigsaw pieces to make the dinosaur's bones and teeth – will have been changed by minerals in the surrounding rock and turned into stone. The cells will still be there, but they will be made of a different material – often the hard mineral **silica**.

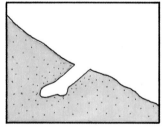

**Mold fossils.** The bones and teeth may rot away slowly, leaving a hole in the rock the exact shape of the original remains. These holes are called **molds**.

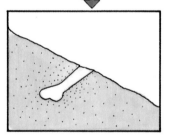

**Cast fossils.** Sometimes, after a mold has formed, different chemicals find their way into the hole and build up. They form a fossil that is exactly the same shape as the original remains, but made of a different material. This is called a **cast**.

## WHOLE ANIMALS

Very rarely, whole animals may be preserved as fossils. One example is an insect in amber. Imagine that, millions of years ago, sap oozed out of the trunk of a fir tree. An insect landed in the sap and became completely covered. Over millions of years, the sap turned into a mineral called amber, and the insect was preserved inside. You can see a spider that has been trapped in amber in the photograph below.

An even rarer example is when a whole animal is frozen, and preserved just like the food in a freezer! Woolly mammoths have been preserved in this way, entombed in the frozen mud of Siberia.

Another way that plants and animals can be preserved is by being turned into the chemical element carbon – the most important one in any living thing. When an animal or plant is buried and compressed, this element may be all that is left behind after millions of years. When this happens to millions and millions of plants all together, the carbon builds up to form a coal seam.

The same thing happens when a plant is burned, but more quickly. If you look at the remains left by a bonfire, you will see that any sticks left have turned to black charcoal. This charcoal is the carbon – all that is left of the wood when the other chemicals have been burned away.

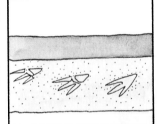

The dinosaur left footprints in the mud on the riverbank. They are baked dry by the sun and become fossilized in the same way as the bones and teeth.

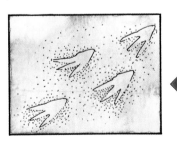

**Trace fossils.** Sometimes, sediments may fill the hollows made by the dinosaur's footprints. These sediments may form rock which is harder than the rock around it. This softer rock washes away, leaving the footprints standing out. These are called **trace fossils**. Scientists sometimes find the fossil of a worm's burrow or an animal's droppings. These are trace fossils, too.

# Where to find fossils

As you know from page 6, sedimentary rocks are laid down in layers. But they do not usually stay like this. The Earth movements that build up mountain ranges can twist and fold sedimentary rocks so that they are no longer flat. When these rocks appear at the surface of the Earth they are called an **outcrop**. You can look for fossils in outcrops of sedimentary rocks.

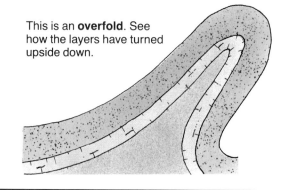

A sea cliff gives a very good outcrop, usually with plenty of rocks exposed. Sea cliffs are being worn away all the time, so be very careful if you go looking for fossils in case loose rocks fall on you. The fallen rocks at the base of a cliff can be good places to find fossils.

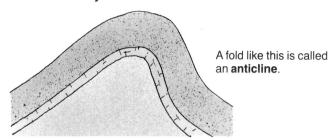

A fold like this is called an **anticline**.

This is an **overfold**. See how the layers have turned upside down.

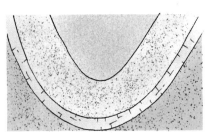

A fold like this is called a **syncline**.

---

# Make your own anticline

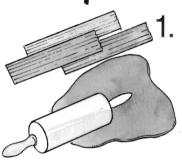

**1.** Take six different colors of Plasticine. These will be your layers of sedimentary rock. Roll and flatten them into strips.

**2.** Put the strips together. One on top of the other. In between the layers sprinkle some grains of sand. These will be your "fossils."

**3.** Now bend your layers of Plasticine into the shape of an anticline.

**4.** By cutting off the highest part of your model, you will see how the different layers of rock are exposed.

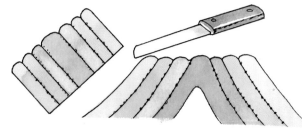

Sometimes human beings make outcrops! They dig up the Earth, searching for stone or minerals, forming quarries. Old limestone quarries can be good fossil sites. Always make sure you get permission before going to such places and watch out for loose or falling rocks. Road and railway cuttings are other good man-made sites to look for fossils.

Stream gullies and river beds cut through rocks and give good outcrops. The best places are usually on the outsides of stream bends. Remember, you should always be careful when you are close to water.

# The fossil hunter's equipment

*When you go looking for fossils, don't take too much equipment. A bag full of heavy specimens is quite enough to carry home!*

You should take a hammer with you for breaking open rocks. A geological hammer with a chisel-like attachment on the head is the best kind to use. Use this for splitting rocks to find the fossils trapped inside. A pair of goggles will protect your eyes against flying chips of stone.

A hand lens is useful. You might find fossils that are too small to see properly with the naked eye.

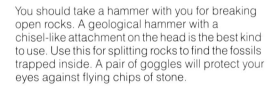

Take a large-scale map of the area you are visiting to show you where quarries, cliffs and other possible fossil sites exist, plus a ruler for measuring the fossils you find.

A camera will be useful for photographing interesting outcrops. This will help you to remember later where you found your fossils.

Number your specimens and wrap them in newspaper before putting them into a sturdy bag.

Make sure that your clothing is suitable for a day out in whatever sort of countryside you are visiting.

You must take a notebook and pencils. As soon as you find something interesting, take a note of where you found it and in what kind of rock.

# Golden rules

**Before you go out on a fossil hunt:**
**a.** Decide where you're going and always get permission to visit any site which is on private land.
**b.** Use a map to plot your route to the destination and back again. Always show an adult where you are going, which way you are going and what time you'll be back.

**Getting ready:**
**a.** Make a list of all equipment needed.
**b.** Check weather forecasts.
**c.** Take a basic first aid kit with you.
**d.** Take some money, just in case you need to make an emergency 'phone call.
**e.** Never go on a fossil hunt alone – take a friend, preferably an adult, with you.

**Out and about:**
*Always put safety first:*
**a.** Do not climb beyond your ability.
**b.** Beware of falling rocks.
**c.** If it is necessary to use a tool to loosen rocks, then wear protective goggles or shield your face with your hand.
**d.** Always beware of water which is cold, deep, tidal or likely to have strong currents.
**e.** Never play near water. If you fall in, it may be a long, cold journey home.
**f.** Look out for information notices and do what they say.

# M king fossils

*Here are some different kinds of fossils. Can you tell from the descriptions* **which one is a petrified fossil, which is a cast fossil and which a trace fossil?**

A. These marks were made as a trilobite skuttled across a sea bed.

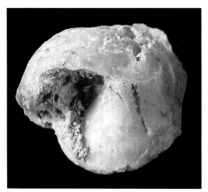

B. The cells of this gastropod have been replaced by silica.

C. After this crab rotted away other sediments filled the hole.

---

# Make an insect in amber

*You can make your own fossil in amber like this:*

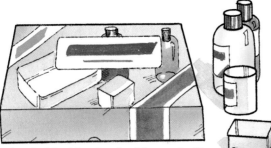

**1.** You can buy hobby kits of embedding resin. The kit will come with the resin, a chemical to harden it, and some molds to make jewelry shapes.

**2.** Mix some resin with a few drops of hardener, then use it to half fill a mould and let it set.

**3.** Now put a dead insect on top of this and pour in another layer of resin and hardener.

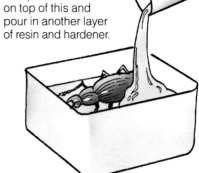

**4.** Once it has set, the block of resin will come out of the mold with the insect preserved inside it — just like the fossil insect in preserved amber.

---

# Make a cast fossil
*You can make a cast fossil like this:*

**1.** Model a small, simple fossil shape out of Plasticine – a shell, bone or tooth would be best.

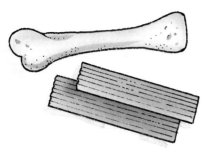

**2.** Find an old plastic or foil container deep enough to take your model – a margarine dish for example. Mix up enough plaster of Paris to half-fill the container. Pour it in. Before it sets, press your model into it.

**3.** Roll out some Plasticine very thinly. Cut it into strips and use these to cover the surface of the plaster of Paris, taking care to fit them round your model as closely as possible. Make sure that they touch the edge of the container too.

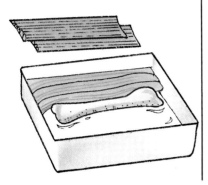

**4.** Mix some more plaster of Paris and pour it over the Plasticine layer, making sure that it covers your model. Let it set.

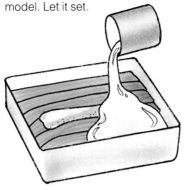

**5.** When it is hard, take the plaster of Paris mold out of the container. Separate the two halves and peel away all the Plasticine, taking care to clean it out of the fossil mold.

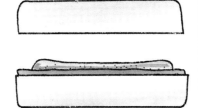

**6.** Dust the inside surface of each half of the fossil shape with talcum powder.

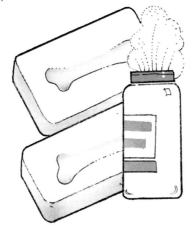

**7.** Take some self-hardening modelling clay or some fresh Plasticine. Knead it into a soft mass, as big as your fossil shape. Press it into one half of your mold. Firmly press the other half of the mold on top, so that the two plaster of Paris halves meet.

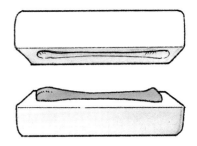

**8.** Gently open the two halves of the mold and take out your fossil cast Neaten the edges. If you use modelling clay, let it harden.

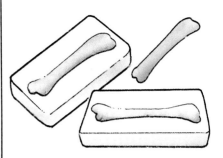

**9.** You now have your own cast 'fossil'.

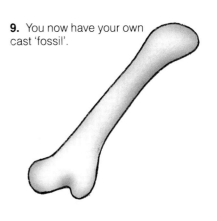

# *Thick-skinned!*

*Arthropods* *are animals that carry their skeletons outside their bodies. Insects are arthropods. So are spiders, scorpions, shrimps, crabs and lobsters. These are all found as fossils. Sometimes their shells are preserved without any change. Sometimes they are petrified. They are also found as molds and casts.*

## TRILOBITES

The most interesting fossil arthropods are the **trilobites**. They lived at the bottom of the sea in the Palaeozoic era. When they were alive they looked like woodlice, with a segmented body, many legs and a triangular tail shield at the end. It is usually this skeleton that is preserved. We hardly ever find the remains of the delicate antennae and legs.

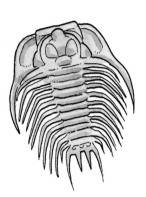

**Agnostus.** This trilobite lived from the Middle Cambrian to the Late Ordovician period. At about ½ an inch long, it was one of the smallest, and probably lived by swimming about and eating microscopic floating animals.

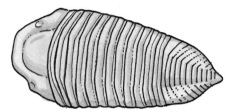

**Trimerus.** This smooth, spade-shaped trilobite lived by burrowing in the sand of the sea bed. It lived during the Middle Silurian period.

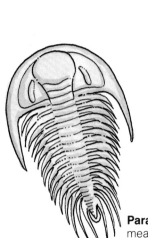

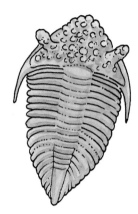

**Encrinurus.** This strange-looking creature had a big round bump at the front of its headshield and eyes on stalks. It lived on the ocean floor during the Late Silurian period.

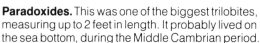

**Acidaspis.** Just over 1 inch long, this trilobite swam above the ocean floor during the Silurian period. It had a very ornate headshield and long spines on its segments.

**Paradoxides.** This was one of the biggest trilobites, measuring up to 2 feet in length. It probably lived on the sea bottom, during the Middle Cambrian period.

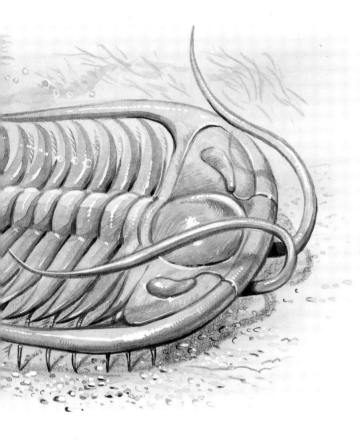

## FOSSIL TRILOBITES

Here are two pictures of fossil trilobites. **Can you guess the names of each one by looking at the fossils on the opposite page?**

The fossil above has a rounded lump on the front of its headshield. Those below are less than ½ an inch long.

# Curling up in fright

*Some trilobites could roll up to defend themselves from their enemies. We can tell this from fossils that have been found curled up in this way.*

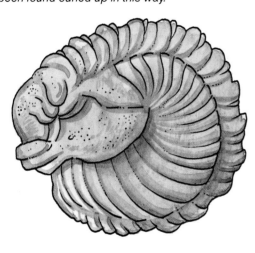

⋆* **ANSWERS** *⋆

The top picture is of a fossil Encrinurus. The bottom picture is of the tiny Agnostus.

# Moving without legs

Some animals can crawl along, even though they do not have any legs. They are called **gastropods**. They usually have a spiral shell. Snails are the gastropods you probably know best. The gastropods that are common as fossils are ones that lived in the sea – like winkles and whelks. We find different gastropods in rocks of different ages.

Gastropod shells can become fossils just as they are, or they can be molds or casts. Often there is a cast of the inside of the shell. This happens where the shell filled up with mud and that mud hardened. These casts make a very graceful shape in the rock. The fossils above are of freshwater gastropods preserved in limestone.

# Gastropod gallery

**Heliconella.** This gastropod lived during the Early Cambrian period. It is similar to today's limpet.

**Poleumita.** This creature, from the Silurian period, had a flat spiral shell with knobs and ridges on one side.

**Viviparus.** This first appeared in the Jurassic period and is still around today. Its fossils are found in rocks made from sediments left by fresh water.

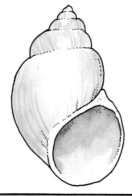

**Murchisonia.** This gastropod lived from the Devonian to the Carboniferous period. It was about 2 inches long.

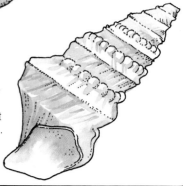

Some animals grow inside a pair of shells. These are called **bivalves**. The two shells are usually mirror images of each other. Most of the seashells you see on the beach today are bivalves. They may have growth lines, like the rings you see inside a tree, or they may have ribs radiating from the point at the top. Bivalves can become fossils just as they are, or as casts or molds. The shells may be fossilized together or separately.

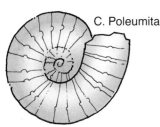

A modern-day bivalve – the common mussel.

**Lopha.** This bivalve had a long curved shell, covered with deep ribs and growth lines, it lived during the late Jurassic and Cretaceous period.

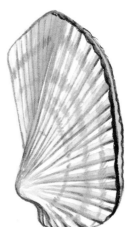

**Parallelodon.** This bivalve lived from the Devonian to the Jurassic period. It had a narrow shell just over 1 inch long.

**Gryphaea.** This was a kind of oyster, about 3 inches long. It lived during the Jurassic period. Unlike most other bivalves, it had two different sized shells – one big and curved like a claw, the other small and fitted in like a lid.

# Which layer?

These three fossils were found in different layers of sedimentary rock. Read the descriptions of each creature and see if you can work out to which layer each belongs.

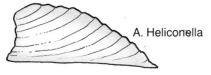

A. Heliconella

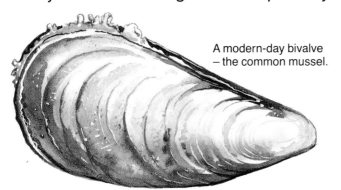

C. Poleumita

B. Gryphaea

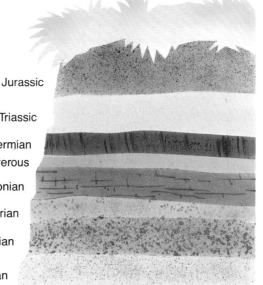

Jurassic

Triassic

Permian

Carboniferous

Devonian

Silurian

Ordivician

Cambrian

# Animals with tentacles

Animals with tentacles are called **cephalopods**. Octopus and squid are both examples of cephalopods which can still be found today. So is the nautilus which looks like an octopus with a coiled shell. In the past a great many cephalopods had shells of one kind or another, and we often find these as fossils.

In cephalopod fossils, the shell is sometimes preserved unaltered. More often, the shell has gone and all we can see is the cast of the inside. The shell may be straight, curved or tightly coiled. As the animal became larger, it grew a wider shell to protect it. Its body moved forwards from the original part of the shell and walled it off. A coiled cephalopod shell is different from the coiled shell of a gastropod because it is divided up into these chambers inside.

## Fossil relatives

Here are some extinct creatures and their modern-day relatives. **Can you put them into pairs according to their animal groups?**

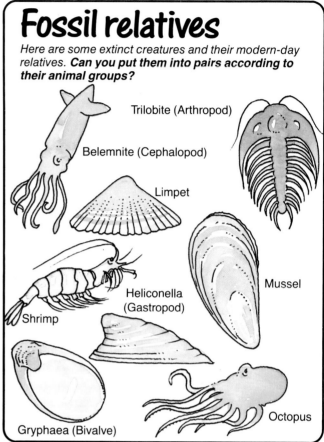

Belemnite (Cephalopod)

Trilobite (Arthropod)

Limpet

Heliconella (Gastropod)

Mussel

Shrimp

Gryphaea (Bivalve)

Octopus

①

③

# Ammonites~short, but important lives

Ammonites were a special group of cephalopods that lived in the Jurassic and Cretaceous periods. There were many of them, and they lived all over the world. They evolved very quickly and each species only lived for a very short time. Because of this they are important to geologists, who use them to date the rocks in which they are found.

Ammonite shells came in many different shapes, and most fossils are up to 2 inches across. You can see some different ammonite shells in this panel.

Fossil ammonite

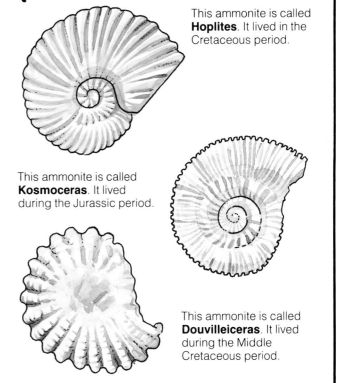

This ammonite is called **Hoplites**. It lived in the Cretaceous period.

This ammonite is called **Kosmoceras**. It lived during the Jurassic period.

This ammonite is called **Douvilleiceras**. It lived during the Middle Cretaceous period.

(2)

*In the picture on the left you can see some different types of cephalopod that are often found as fossils.*

**1. Orthoceras** was a nautiloid, a straight-shelled relative of today's nautilus. It was a fast-moving hunter and could grow to nearly 10 feet in length.

**2. Belemnites** were very common during the Jurassic and Cretaceous periods. They had rows of tiny hooks on their tentacles to catch their prey. Their hard bullet-shaped shell is all we normally find as fossils.

**3. Goniatites** had tightly coiled shells and were similar to the ammonites above. They could grow to 1½ inches in diameter and lived during the Carboniferous period.

# Spiny skins

**Echinoderms** are spiny-skinned animals. There are still plenty around today. We call them starfish, brittle stars and sea urchins.

Starfish break up when they die, so we do not often find them as fossils. Fossil urchins are more common. Differently-shaped sea urchins had different lifestyles. Round flat ones crawled along the sea bed. Heart-shaped ones burrowed in the sand. Most sea urchins had "arm areas." These were rows of holes, through which little tentacles could poke. Most urchins were also covered in spines, but these are not often fossilized.

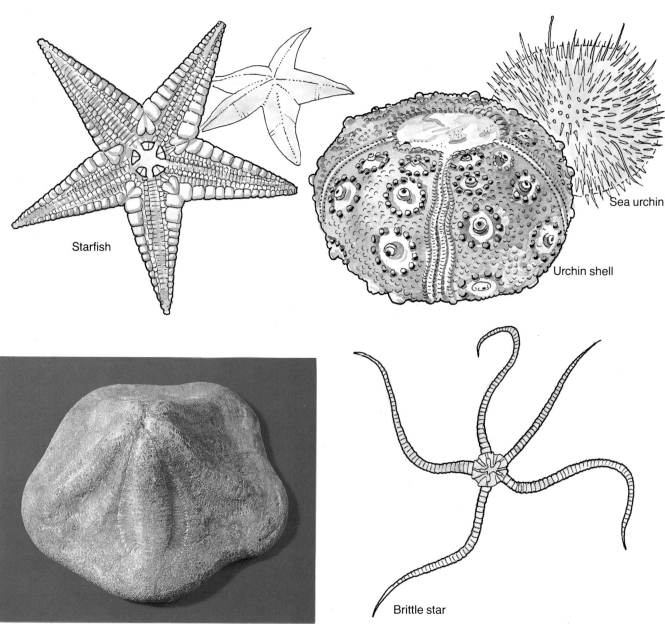

Starfish

Sea urchin

Urchin shell

This fossil sea urchin has lost its spines.

Brittle star

# Corals

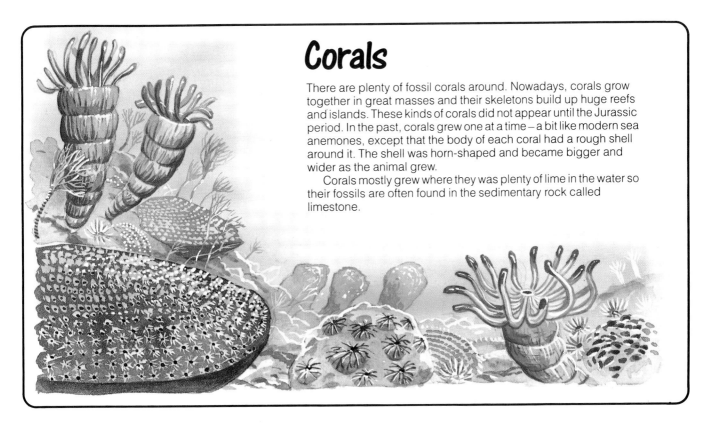

There are plenty of fossil corals around. Nowadays, corals grow together in great masses and their skeletons build up huge reefs and islands. These kinds of corals did not appear until the Jurassic period. In the past, corals grew one at a time – a bit like modern sea anemones, except that the body of each coral had a rough shell around it. The shell was horn-shaped and became bigger and wider as the animal grew.

Corals mostly grew where they was plenty of lime in the water so their fossils are often found in the sedimentary rock called limestone.

## THE SEA LILY

The sea lily is a very common echinoderm fossil. Imagine a starfish on a stalk- that's a sea lily. They are not common today but they were plentiful in the past. Sometimes they grew together in thick forests under the sea. Limestone rock is sometimes made up entirely of sea lily stalks.

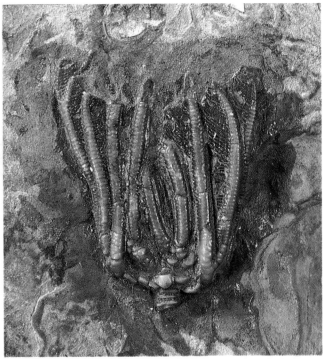

Fossil sea lily

# Sitting on the sea bed

If you saw a live **brachiopod** you would probably think it was a bivalve. Brachiopods are about the same size as bivalves and they also have two shells. However, there is a totally different animal inside. Brachiopods and bivalves look like one another because they have the same lifestyle. They sit and filter food at the bottom of the sea, and they need hard shells to protect themselves.

This fossil brachiopod comes from the Silurian period.

## Mysterious fossils

Use this chart to identify these eight mystery creatures.

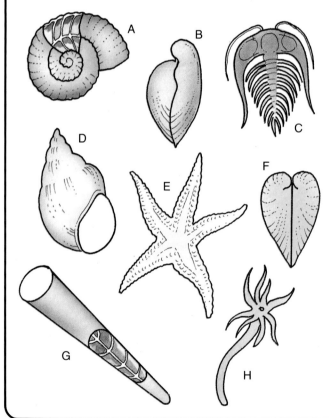

**★ ANSWERS ★**

A is an ammonite.
B is a brachiopod.
C is a trilobite.

D is a gastropod.
E is a starfish.
F is a bivalve.
G is a belemnite.
H is a sea lily.

# A bivalve or a brachiopod?

If you find two halves of a brachiopod shell together, it is easy to tell the difference between it and a bivalve.

Turn the shell sideways so that you can see the join between the two shells. Imagine a line being drawn along this join from top to bottom. If your specimen is a bivalve the shells each side of this line will be the same size.

If the two halves do not match, one of them is smaller than the other, and acts like a lid, then you have a brachiopod.

A living brachiopod has a coiled tentacle inside. It uses this to gather small pieces of food from sea water that passes through its shell when it is open. A brachiopod usually has a foot as well. This grows through a hole in one of the shells, and is used to attach the animal to a rock.

Brachiopod

Bivalve

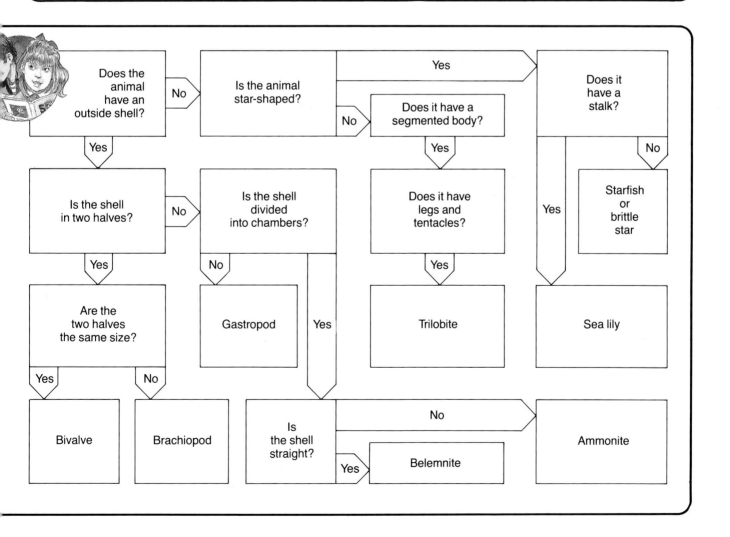

Does the animal have an outside shell? — No → Is the animal star-shaped? — Yes → Does it have a stalk?

Is the animal star-shaped? — No → Does it have a segmented body?

Does it have a stalk? — No → Starfish or brittle star

Does the animal have an outside shell? — Yes → Is the shell in two halves?

Is the shell in two halves? — No → Is the shell divided into chambers?

Does it have a segmented body? — Yes → Does it have legs and tentacles?

Does it have a stalk? — Yes → Sea lily

Is the shell in two halves? — Yes → Are the two halves the same size?

Is the shell divided into chambers? — No → Gastropod

Does it have legs and tentacles? — Yes → Trilobite

Are the two halves the same size? — Yes → Bivalve

Are the two halves the same size? — No → Brachiopod

Is the shell divided into chambers? — Yes → Is the shell straight?

Is the shell straight? — No → Ammonite

Is the shell straight? — Yes → Belemnite

# Too small to see

Some fossils are so small that they cannot be seen with the naked eye. They have to be looked at through a microscope. They are called **microfossils**.

Microfossils are very important to scientists searching for oil trapped deep in the Earth's crust. By studying the microfossils in the small examples of rock brought up by the oil drills, they can tell what the rocks are like, and if they are likely to contain oil.

Here you can see some common microfossils, as they would appear under the microscope.

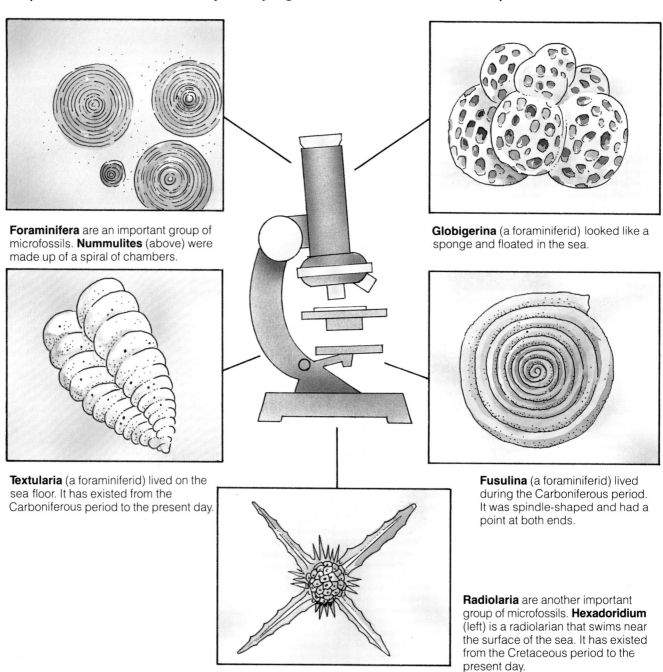

**Foraminifera** are an important group of microfossils. **Nummulites** (above) were made up of a spiral of chambers.

**Globigerina** (a foraminiferid) looked like a sponge and floated in the sea.

**Textularia** (a foraminiferid) lived on the sea floor. It has existed from the Carboniferous period to the present day.

**Fusulina** (a foraminiferid) lived during the Carboniferous period. It was spindle-shaped and had a point at both ends.

**Radiolaria** are another important group of microfossils. **Hexadoridium** (left) is a radiolarian that swims near the surface of the sea. It has existed from the Cretaceous period to the present day.

## THE CONODONTS

The **conodonts** have always been a puzzling group of microfossils. The only remains ever found looked like tiny jaw bones with lots of teeth. Recently scientists have discovered that these jaw bones actually belonged to an animal that looked like a worm with a fish's tail! Conodonts are very useful to geologists – if a rock contains their fossils then we know it was formed during the Palaeozoic era.

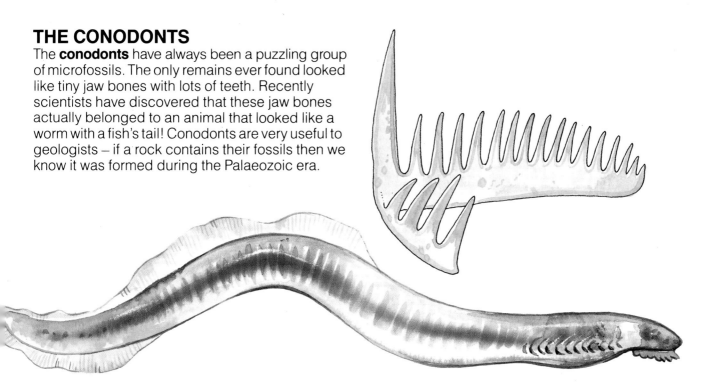

# Living together

**Graptolites** were not microfossils but their fossils can still be difficult to see – sometimes they just look like pencil marks on the rock.

When alive, the individual graptolites looked like tiny corals, but they lived together in great bunches, called colonies, that looked more like large jellyfish! Sometimes these bunches were stuck to driftwood, sometimes they floated freely in the sea. When they died, they sank into the depths of the sea and became fossils.

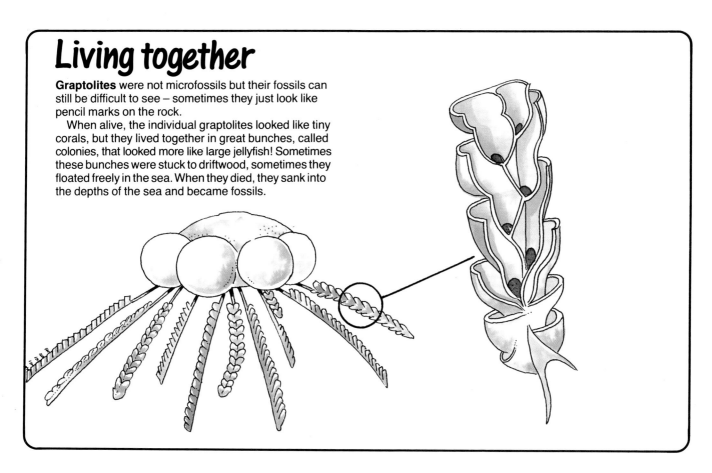

# *Rare finds*

*Some of the most spectacular fossils are those of the **vertebrates**, or animals with backbones. Most fish, and all birds and mammals (including you and I) are vertebrates. So were the dinosaurs.*

*Unfortunately, you are unlikely to find any fossil remains of these creatures. They are very rare. However, you might, if you are very lucky, find a piece of backbone or a fish's tooth.*

# Whole skeletons

Dinosaur skeletons like this are very important and rare finds for the fossil detective. By piecing together the remains, scientists can tell a great deal about how a dinosaur lived, what it ate and, sometimes, what the world in which it lived was like.

This picture (right) shows the skeleton of a **Psittacosaurus** with its distinctive parrot-shaped beak. It grew to a length of over 6 feet and has been discovered in Asia in layers of rock from the Cretaceous Period.

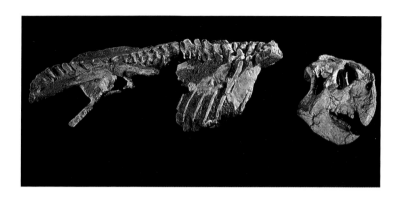

This is the tooth of a prehistoric fish called **acrodus**. Scientists can tell that this fish ate shellfish by looking at the shape of its tooth which is broad and flat for crushing.

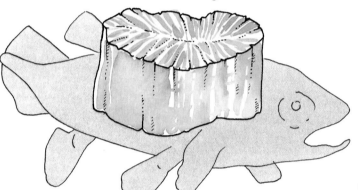

Shark's tooth from the Cretaceous period. We can tell from its pointed, saw-edged shape that this creature ate fish.

## WHO TROD HERE?

This fossilized dinosaur footprint is over 100 million years old. Trace fossils of the dinosaurs – especially their footprints – are more common than the remains of the animals themselves. A dinosaur will have left millions of footprints in its lifetime, but only one skeleton!

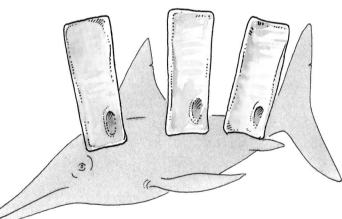

Segment of the backbone of a fish-lizard called **ichthyosaurus**. This strange creature lived during the Jurassic and Cretaceous periods.

# Fossil get-together

You hardly ever find a single fossil by itself. The reason is this. Imagine the bottom of the sea. Many of the creatures we have described are living there. Then a fierce wind sweeps sand into the water and buries them. They are all killed immediately. These creatures will eventually become a huge fossil collection, trapped in rock.

Imagine, too, a river in flood. The rainwater washes off the land, carrying dead land animals and trees with it. The flooded river washes all these down to the sea. The weather that has caused the flood has caused a storm at sea as well. Big waves are pounding the beach, dislodging bivalves and tearing apart sea urchins and sea lilies. Then, when the storm dies down, the debris settles at the bottom of the sea to eventually become another fossil collection.

The fossils of the sea animals buried by sand will show how the creatures were living the moment they died. The bivalves will be in their burrows, with their two shells still joined. Sea lilies and sea urchins will still be whole, as will prehistoric fish and other sea creatures. The geologist calls this collection of fossils a **life assemblage**. It is important because it shows us how creatures lived long ago.

The assemblage caused by the storm will reveal dead land animals and plants, bivalves that have come apart and sea urchins in pieces – all mixed up together. This mixture of fossil remains is called a **death assemblage**. It does not tell us much about the living conditions of the animals it contains.

# Phoney fossils

Watch out for phoney fossils! These are not fakes that someone has put together to mislead us. They are natural formations that look a bit like fossils, but are not. We call them **pseudofossils**.

When minerals form in a rock they usually form crystals that have straight edges. But sometimes they form knobbly shapes, like this one, that look like the fossilised remains of a strange creature. Iron ore often forms shapes like this. We call it "**kidney ore**."

The white sedimentary rock called chalk is full of rounded lumps of the mineral silica. These lumps are called **flints**. They may form very strange shapes, sometimes looking like fossil bones.

These are **dendrites**. They look like the small, dark remains of a prehistoric plant, but they are really mineral deposits left by water seeping through cracks in the rock. Some dendrites look like pieces of moss trapped in rock,. They are sometimes used in jewelry and are then called "moss agates."

# Fossils at work

*It is interesting to find a fossil trapped in stone – the remains of an animal which has been buried unseen for millions and millions of years, until your hammer splits the stone open. It is fascinating to think about what these strange animals looked like when they were alive. But are fossils any use to us?*

## Breaking up!

Sometimes geologists find the same type of sedimentary rock – containing the same fossils, and the same number and thicknesses of layers – miles and miles apart. This can sometimes indicate that the two pieces of rock were once joined. For example, parts of Africa and America contain very similar rocks and fossils which make scientists think that the two countries were once part of one gigantic land mass that was broken up by movements in the Earth's crust.

## USEFUL FOSSILS
A seam of coal is one big fossil – the fossil of a forest! We have seen how a leaf can be preserved as a thin film of carbon (see page 11). Imagine this happening to millions of leaves. That is how coal is formed. Most coal was formed from the forests of giant fern trees and other plants that grew during the Carboniferous period. Coal is an important fuel.

## FOSSIL CLUES
Geologists can use fossils to date the ages of rocks. They can work out how old a rock layer is by looking at the type of fossils it contains. Some fossils are particularly suitable for this, such as the graptolite shown above, because the creatures that formed them only existed for a short time. Fossils like this are called "index" fossils.

Oil is a very important fuel, too. It is formed from the bodies of millions of tiny sea creatures whose remains fell to the bottom of an ancient ocean and became compressed into oil over millions of years. To find the oil, geologists examine likely rocks on the look-out for certain kinds of fossil. These fossils are usually only found in the rocks surrounding pockets of oil. We call both oil and coal **fossil fuels.**

Limestone is often made almost entirely of fossils. It can be made up of fossil corals or shells all jammed together, or microfossils that are too small to see. Like many other sedimentary rocks such as sandstone, limestone is used for building, and in the manufacture of cement. The lime is also extracted from it and used as a fertilizer and in the chemical industry.

# Fossil detectives

Without fossils we would know very little about the Earth's past and the creatures that once lived here. From the evidence left behind in the rocks, scientists have been able to piece together the history of life on our planet. By comparing fossil skeletons with those of creatures which exist today, fossil detectives can tell us about the animals that once roamed the Earth – what they looked like, what they ate, where and how they lived. Without fossils none of this would have been possible.

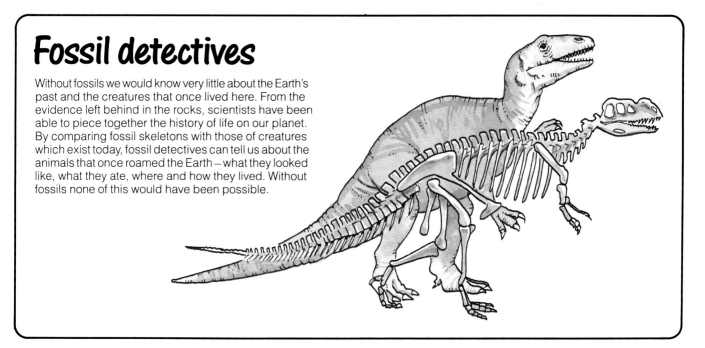

# *Fossil plants*

The flowering plants that we know today did not evolve until the Cretaceous period. Conifers (firs and pines) are a little older. They have been around since the Permian period.

Before that, there were all kinds of strange trees. Some were related to the ferns, others were related to the tiny fern-like plants we call club-mosses.

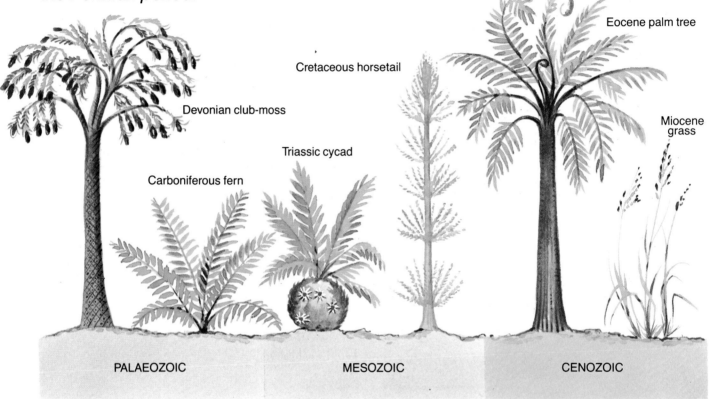

Cretaceous horsetail

Eocene palm tree

Devonian club-moss

Miocene grass

Triassic cycad

Carboniferous fern

PALAEOZOIC

MESOZOIC

CENOZOIC

A fossil leaf from the Tertiary period

Fossil ferns from the Carboniferous period

# A trip to the coal bunker

If there is a coal fire in your house, you need not go far to look for fossils. Just go to where the coal is kept and try splitting open some lumps of coal. Sometimes you can see the shapes of fern leaves and pieces of wood in the coal.

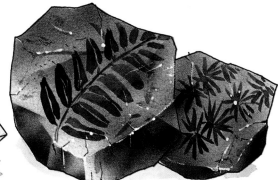

# Fossil collections

Making your own fossil collection can be great fun. You can use this book as a rough guide to fossil types but, if you find any that you can't identify, look for books in bookshops and libraries that may help you. You can also visit your local museum. They may have a similar fossil on display. If not, there may be somebody there who can help you identify your find.

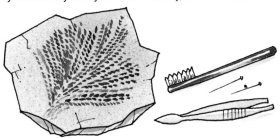

**1.** The first thing to do with your fossils, once you get them safely home, is to clean them thoroughly. An old toothbrush is ideal for cleaning away soft shale or clay from a fossil. A pin and a pair of tweezers will also be useful – but be careful of sharp points! Remember to handle your fossils very carefully – many will break easily.

**3.** Put your cleaned fossils in an open-topped box or drawer, each one labelled with its name and number. Now you can start a catalogue. In a notebook or card file, write down all the details you know about each fossil in numbered order – where it was found, what it is etc. You could also do a drawing of it, and a drawing showing what the creature was like when it was alive.

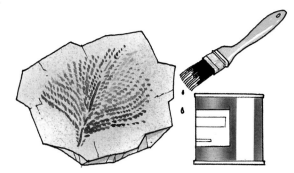

**2.** If the fossil is a very fragile one, such as a graptolite, it is best to leave it with its rock surround. Coat the whole thing with shellac or a similar varnish. This will make it stronger, and will also preserve the color of the original rock.

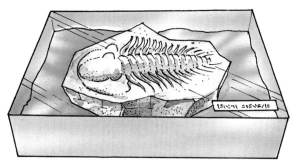

**4.** A really good or unusual specimen deserves special treatment. Put it on display, perhaps in a transparent plastic box, on a piece of velvet.

# Quiz time

## HOW LONG AGO?

Here are pictures of two ancient sea beds. Look at the animals that are living there. **Can you tell in what period the scenes are set?**

A

Acidaspis

Trimerus

Poleumita

B

Ichthyosaurus

Belemnite

Parallelodon

Kosmoceras

36

# How old are the rocks?

Here is a sequence of sedimentary rocks which have been disturbed by earth movements. **Using the fossils, can you work out which layer is the youngest and which the oldest?**

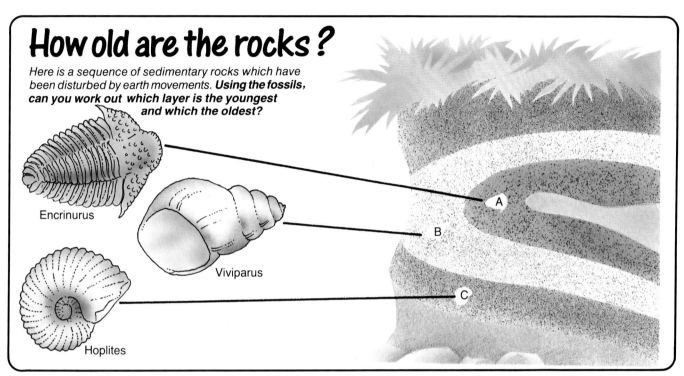

Encrinurus

Viviparus

Hoplites

A

B

C

## BIVALVE OR BRACHIOPOD?

Here are some fossil shellfish. Some are bivalves and some are brachiopods. **Can you tell which are which?**

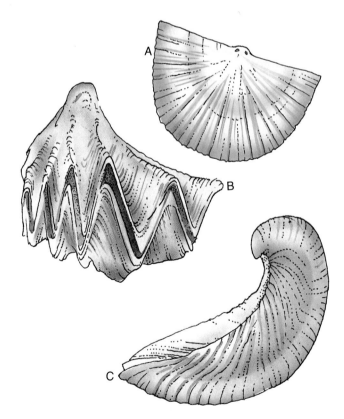

A

B

C

37

# Index